My First Lohri

Chandan Bhogal

AuthorHouse™ UK
1663 Liberty Drive
Bloomington, IN 47403 USA
www.authorhouse.co.uk
UK TFN: 0800 0148641 (Toll Free inside the UK)
UK Local: 02036 956322 (+44 20 3695 6322 from outside the UK)

Because of the dynamic nature of the Internet, any web addresses or links contained in this book may have changed since publication and may no longer be valid. The views expressed in this work are solely those of the author and do not necessarily reflect the views of the publisher, and the publisher hereby disclaims any responsibility for them.

Any people depicted in stock imagery provided by Getty Images are models, and such images are being used for illustrative purposes only.
Certain stock imagery © Getty Images.

This book is printed on acid-free paper.

ISBN: 978-1-6655-9739-5 (sc)
ISBN: 978-1-6655-9740-1 (e)

Print information available on the last page.

Published by AuthorHouse 05/16/2022

authorHOUSE®

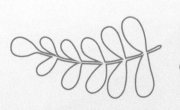

Introduction

As a recent father of a beautiful baby girl, I created a few short stories and poems to help entertain my daughter. Friends and family liked the stories and told me to get them published.

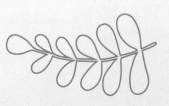

The time has come to perform
the ritual for your first Lohri,
friends, family, everyone.

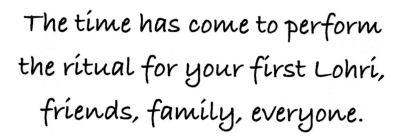

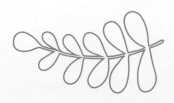

Bonfires are lit to mark the harvest festival occasion. We dance and sing around it in joyous celebration.

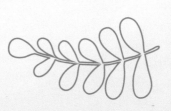

We throw sugarcane, popcorn and sticks on the fire. We wear brightly coloured clothing. It is a festival to celebrate the end of winter and welcome the new year.

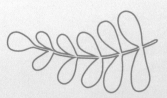

We fill our tummies with
things we love, such as dhal,
saag, kheer, roti, and gobi.

As the day drifts to night, the flames get lower. Everyone leaves as it comes to an end. Happy new year until it's time for Lohri again.

The End

Printed in the United States
by Baker & Taylor Publisher Services